T0016596

THE
GHOSTLY TALES
OF
THE
PACIFIC
NORTHWEST

Published by Arcadia Children's Books
A Division of Arcadia Publishing
Charleston, SC
www.arcadiapublishing.com

Spooky America is a trademark of Arcadia Publishing, Inc.

First published 2022

Manufactured in the United States

ISBN 978-1-4671-9873-8

Library of Congress Control Number: 2022932233

All images courtesy of Shutterstock.com; p. 22 Ritu Manoj Jethani/Shutterstock.com.

Notice: The information in this book is true and complete to the best of our
knowledge. It is offered without guarantee on the part of the author or Arcadia
Publishing. The author and Arcadia Publishing disclaim all liability in connection with
the use of this book.

Spooky America

THE GHOSTLY TALES OF

THE PACIFIC NORTHWEST

DEBORAH CUYLE

Adapted from *Haunted Graveyard of the Pacific* by Ira Wesley Kitmacher

arcadia
CHILDREN'S BOOKS

BRITISH COLUMBIA

7

6

WASHINGTON

4

5

3

MT

2

1

OREGON

ID

CA

NV

TABLE OF CONTENTS & MAP KEY

Introduction

The Pacific Northwest is a region of the United States that reaches from the Pacific Ocean to the Rocky Mountains, and many of its locations are haunted by creepy ghosts! This book is going to focus on frightening places in Oregon, Washington, and British Columbia. If you have the opportunity to visit any of these spooky locations, you better be prepared to experience quite a thrill! Otherwise, nestle into a comfy chair or snuggle up on the sofa and try to imagine these places in your mind. I guarantee you will get goosebumps from these stories!

In this book, you will read about all kinds of scary stuff: everything from haunted, dark and gloomy towns to creepy ghost ships! Ghosts or spirits can take many shapes and forms; everything from wispy fog to glowing orbs of light to full-body apparitions. If you ever thought you saw a ghost, you would not be alone! Many people believe they have seen or heard a ghost, but what exactly is a ghost?

Are they the spirits of those who once walked the earth, and after they died, they refused to move on? Are they somehow trapped on Earth for a reason, possibly staying due to unfinished business? Or is it simply because they loved their home or family too much to ever leave them?

What do you think? Shall we begin?

Haunted Oregon

We begin our journey in Oregon, at one of the most haunted places in the entire Northwest—a watery graveyard where countless ships, captains, and sailors lost their lives, swallowed up by the sea.

If you can, imagine yourself on a huge ship with the freezing ocean spraying saltwater up and over the hull. As the vessel rocks back and forth fighting treacherous waves, you realize with fear that the boat is caught in a series of deathly currents. Those currents have a name, for those who dare to speak of it.

THE HAUNTED GRAVEYARD OF THE PACIFIC

The Graveyard of the Pacific begins where the Columbia River flows into the Pacific Ocean— roughly from Tillamook Bay (Oregon) all the way north to Cape Scott Provincial Park on Vancouver Island (British Columbia). This is where these two waterways meet and churn with violent currents.

The most dangerous section of the graveyard is called the Columbia Bar. It is near a series of treacherous sandbars. Since the fifteenth century, the deadly combination of these somewhat hidden sandbars, strong unpredictable currents, and extremely thick fog has sent thousands of ships and hundreds of souls to their watery deaths.

One such crew encountered brutal waves while aboard the ship *Anna Anderson*, and their untimely fates are still a mystery today. In January 1869, the men were bringing up a large load of oysters from San Francisco when they met up with sea trouble. The crew met a severe storm, and all seven men and their captain, W.H. Stapleford, vanished at sea, never to be found.

Another tragic story of the ocean stealing souls is of the vessel called the *Sunshine*. What was left of her came floating up onto the shore, bottoms up, on November 22, 1875. The entire crew, all twenty-five men, were missing! No corpses or any cargo were ever found. Some claim the *Sunshine* was swallowed by a sea monster. Even today, sailors traveling the area fear for their lives and pray for a safe docking ashore. Many claim to experience strange occurrences while aboard ships, and they believe the ghostly spirits of the dead sailors still linger in the waves, trapped on the ocean's floor. When on land, they still feel like they are being haunted by those who have been killed by the cruel sea.

In the old days, men would kidnap other men and force them to work on ships against their will. This was called "being shanghaied," a horrible crime inflicted on many unsuspecting men. Maybe their angry spirits still haunt the nearby coastal towns. Others believe the restless spirits are those of lonely lighthouse keepers of the past, who refuse to leave their beautiful homes that provided a guiding light to so many sailors. Still, others believe that hauntings are caused by men who lost their

 valuable gold and cargos in the Graveyard of the Pacific Northwest. Some captains had secret treasure chests

aboard their ships before they went down, and there was no way to save the gold during the chaos of a shipwreck. With the loss of thousands of ships and hundreds of men, there is bound to be a lot of lost treasures and gold sitting on the ocean's floor! Are the ghost sailors and the spirits of pirates still trying to retrieve their plunder from their watery graves? It would be amazing to be able to dive down there and find old coins and treasures. But, although some have tried, the area is far too unsafe and treacherous for any divers to recover any riches.

HAUNTINGS FROM THE SEA

The murky, deep waters of the Columbia near Astoria have been the focus of many ghost stories and legends over the years. The unpredictable waters in the area have capsized over 2,000 ships dating back as far as 1792! The skeletons of the dead sit beside their capsized vessels and sunken treasures, their personal stories now long forgotten.

The sinking of the American steamship SS *General Warren* on January 31, 1852, was a tragedy to be remembered throughout the ages. Records are unclear, but the *Warren* was most likely loaded with livestock and wheat, and as many as seventy passengers, including Captain Charles Thompson and his crew. It was sailing from Portland to San Francisco when the sea began tossing the boat around during an oncoming storm. The vessel was almost 80 years old and already considered unseaworthy.

Initially, Captain George Flavel was at the helm, in charge of maneuvering the *Warren* safely thru the channel. The storm was getting worse by the minute, and he believed it was much too dangerous to continue with the passage. But impatient passengers demanded the journey proceed as planned. Flavel returned to nearby shores hoping for their safety while Captain Thompson assumed command of the boat.

The next morning, word was received that the *Warren* was in trouble. Strong winds held the vessel in its tight grip, so Flavel and a group of men boarded a pilot charter and set out to assist the *Warren*. Yet the storm continued to wail and pulling the *Warren* back to town was not a possibility. The experienced Captain Flavel decided that the best thing to do was to beach the ship on the nearby Clatsop Spit and wait out the storm.

But as skilled as Flavel was, the waves and weather had other plans. It seemed clear the fragile ship would soon be doomed. As the passengers were ordered to huddle together at the front of the ship, Flavel and nine men boarded a small boat and headed back to secure additional assistance for the *Warren*.

By time Flavel returned with the crew of the ship *George and Martha* to assist in the rescue efforts, it was too late. The *Warren* and everything on board had sunk to the bottom. Only two bodies ever washed ashore—a newlywed couple that supposedly drifted onto the sandy beach, still holding hands.

In 1854, the massive stern of the SS *Warren* washed ashore 60 miles away from where it sank. Local legends claim that the many people who perished on the *Warren* still haunt the area, hoping to be rescued from the watery depths below. Late at night, their cries of anguish can be heard over the never-ending roar of the ocean's waves. Can you imagine how spooky it would be to be on a ship with freezing water coming up and in over the sides, knowing your chances of living were slim? The panic, fright, and death involved in a shipwreck could certainly trap the souls of many ghosts, only for them to haunt the area later.

THE DOOMED VOYAGE OF THE *PACIFIC*

Built in New York City in 1850, the *Pacific* was once a magnificent seaworthy boat that weighed 876 tons and was 223 feet long! After years of service, it was left to rot in 1872 near San Francisco. But the gold rush of 1874 resurrected the vessel, and men labored to bring the *Pacific* back to life.

On November 4, 1874, hundreds of people, horses, and buggies were crammed aboard the *Pacific*, heading from Victoria, British Columbia, to San Francisco, California. The ship was crammed overcapacity, and people had to sleep on the floor, elbow to elbow. Manned by Captain J.D. Howell, who was said to be inexperienced, the voyage was soon to be its final one.

While at sea, the ship began taking in water and tilting off to one side as the crew tried in vain to correct the problem. As the *Pacific* sailed around Cape Flattery, it somehow crashed into the *Orpheus*, who was sailing nearby. The *Orpheus* suffered only slight damage, but the *Pacific* began falling apart within minutes. The terrified passengers and crew were frantic to save themselves from drowning. The *Pacific* broke into two sections and quickly sank to the ocean floor, dragging the horses, supplies, cash, crew, and passengers down with it! This wreck is considered one of the worst sea tragedies in Pacific Coast history—over five hundred lives were lost.

People who live in the area claim they sometimes see the ghost ship *Pacific* off in the foggy distance. Those who happen to be in the water as the ghost ship passes say they can smell a putrid odor and hear the eerie moans and cries of the invisible, drowning passengers.

THE POSSESSED SCHOONER *J.C. COUSINS*

The glorious, sixty-six-foot schooner was built in 1863 in San Francisco and used as a private yacht for many years. The handsome woodwork and details made sailing on it a luxurious and marvelous journey. But in 1881, possibly due to financial woes, the *Cousins* became one of two pilot boats that were hired to help maneuver ships through the dangerous Columbia River bar.

One gloomy day on October 6, 1883, the four-man crew of the *J.C. Cousins* left Astoria in search of ships that needed its assistance. None were nearby, so it continued to wait. Then, for some unknown reason, the *Cousins* started making its way out toward the most dangerous section of the bar, and began making laps between the two points, which was strange, as no other boats were around.

Onlookers at shore watched the *Cousins* with mild curiosity until it happened a second time. And then another lap after that. The curious trips back and forth continued all night.

In the morning, nervous bystanders watched from the shore. Their excitement peaked as they watched the *Cousins* begin rushing toward them, but soon, they could not believe their eyes, as the ship slammed itself onto the sand.

Everyone was worried and wanted to help the crew, but it was high tide, and there was no way to safely get out to the *Cousins*. When the low tide finally arrived, citizens rushed to the

boat to help. As they climbed onto the deck, they discovered that there was *no one on board.* No captain had ever been steering the boat back and forth! The ship had been steering itself, risking sinking to the depths below, seemingly possessed by a demon.

No bodies of the crew were ever found, and explanations of what happened are far and wide. Some locals claimed a man on board named Mr. Zeiber had been hired to murder the crew. Others were certain the crew was

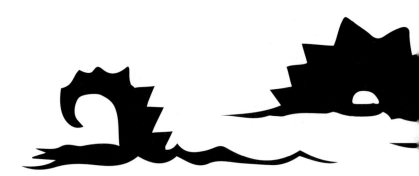

swallowed up by a sea monster! Still, others believed that the *Cousins* had been chased by an invisible ghost ship that stole the men from its deck.

The mystery of the *J.C. Cousins* is unsolved to this day, but it was not the only ship to have sunk in the graveyard mysteriously with no trace of the captain, crew, or sometimes even the ship. Wherever these men vanished to, their ghostly spirits are said to be still trying to find their way ashore to safety.

The Beautiful and Forbidden City of Roses

If you have ever been to Portland, Oregon, you would know how gorgeous the city is. It is also called the "City of Roses." Georgina Pittock, wife to publisher of the *Oregonian*, Henry Pittock, loved roses and soon involved her friends in planting the non-native flower. In 1889, the Portland Rose Society was created, and now thousands of roses adorn the entire city. Over three million people live in Portland—that's almost half of the folks who live in Oregon State. People have been migrating to Portland since the 1840s, when pioneers came via the Oregon Trail. Portland is conveniently situated between the Columbia and Willamette Rivers. It is a bustling hub for cargo ships, trains, and supply trucks.

But hidden within all this beauty is a darker side of Portland. With its sinister and ruthless history full of mobsters, sea captains, and hoodlums, the town's past is perfect for a scary tale or two. After a while, Portland became one of the most dangerous cities in the world: so it was nicknamed the "Forbidden City."

Portland is certainly spooky. So let's explore the City of Roses, shall we? One haunt at a time!

White Eagle Saloon and Hotel

Another hotel in Portland that is full of ghosts is the White Eagle Saloon and Hotel on Russel Street. Since 1905, it has been home to a lot of ghosts. It was a popular watering hole for sailors and dock men who liked to fight. Bloody and violent brawls would happen right in front of the hotel, so it was nicknamed the "Bucket of Blood" hotel.

The most active ghost is named Sam Warrick. Sam lived in the hotel for over forty years, right up until the day he died. He liked to serve food and drinks and fix things that were broken. His picture still hangs on the wall. He can be seen in the kitchen, overlooking the cooks. And if he doesn't think the cooks are doing a great job, he will throw a bottle of ketchup or mustard at them!

A female ghost named Rose likes to linger on the second floor of the White Eagle. She worked at the hotel when she was alive. She died of a broken heart. Rose was in love with a sailor, but the sailor was already married. The unknown sailor went on a long journey, and when he returned to Portland, he sadly discovered that Rose had been murdered! Her apparition can be seen staring out the top story window, still searching for her beloved sailor. The sound of her crying can be heard late at night. Maybe someday Rose will leave the White Eagle, but until then, she continues to roam the place.

THE HAUNTED BENSON HOTEL

The Benson Hotel was built in 1913 and holds almost three hundred beautiful rooms. Towering twelve stories tall, it is a spectacular place to stay the night if you dare. Many ghosts haunt the Benson Hotel. One is the owner himself, Simon Benson, who died in 1942.

When he was alive, he loved his hotel so much, he often told guests that he *never* wanted to leave it. And Mr. Benson kept his word! His spirit is often seen dressed in a sharp, black suit wandering the hotel. He moves people's drinks, "speaks up" during meetings, and "floats" up and down the big stairwell on the main floor. If you ever get to visit the Benson Hotel, keep a keen eye out for Simon; maybe he will even take the time to shake your hand.

The second ghost is a little boy who is three years old with brown hair. Nobody knows his name. He is usually seen sitting by female guests. One lady reported that she woke up to see a little boy standing next to the bed. Although she was startled, she wasn't scared because the boy looked so kind. He even reached out to her! She reached back and could *feel* his arm! After a few seconds, his spirit slowly faded away. When she went to the lobby the next morning, she was surprised to find that several other guests had also experienced seeing the ghost of the little boy.

An older male ghost can be seen working on things, fiddling with objects, and straightening linens. The hotel believes that he is the spirit of a former hotel porter who loved his job so much, he still wants to make sure the guests

have the perfect stay! Visitors sometimes hear old ballroom music and voices when no one else is in the room. Shadowy figures are seen lurking in the halls and the backs of rooms.

PIZZA AND A GHOST, ANYONE?

If your two favorite things are pizza and ghosts, then you are in luck! Old Town Pizza on Davis Street offers the best pizza *and* ghost tours! Located over the old and spooky shanghai tunnels, it offers tours of its haunted basement and the tunnels. The building was once the Merchant Hotel, built in 1880 by two men who made a bunch of money selling lumber.

The ghost that has lived there for over 100 years is a young girl named Nina. She used to work at the Merchant. She also had a 12-year-old daughter, whom she loved very much and was trying to raise by herself. One couple felt sorry for Nina, so they told her they could help make her and her daughter more comfortable. Nina found all of this very exciting, and she started to make plans for her new life.

But that didn't happen. Nina was found dead at the bottom of the elevator shaft.

Did someone push her?

Was it an accident?

Her daughter was never found, and now they both haunt the building, the only place they ever really called home. People hear a woman crying and see a ghost wearing a long black dress. She has long, black hair and is very light in complexion. Is Nina crying because she cannot find her daughter? A young girl's laughter can be heard, as well, like she is playing hide and seek. Sometimes, the fragrance of Nina's perfume can be smelled. Several people have said when they visit the women's bathroom, they look up to see Nina staring right at them!

THE MYSTERIOUS SHANGHAI TUNNELS

Portland has a large area near the Burnside Bridge that is known as "Chinatown," which has a storied past. Large ships would come to port to sell their imports from all over the world: luxurious silk, exotic spices, and beautiful art pieces. Hundreds of people flocked to the docks when the ships arrived, hoping to buy the best wares.

But best beware: bad captains lurked all about waiting to "shanghai" unfortunate souls. Imagine being held captive aboard a huge ship with no way to escape! Some believe that underground tunnels were used by these cruel men. Even today, if you are walking along a sidewalk in Portland and see purple glass squares in the cement, that means there are tunnels below your feet.

One notorious kidnapper was Bunko Kelly. Bunko kidnapped thousands of people to work on ships, starting in 1879. Once Bunko's men grabbed their victims, they would drop them through a trap door in the ship. When the prisoners woke up, they discovered they had been sold as a slave! Bunko continued kidnapping and selling people (it wasn't against the law back then) until about 1895, when he killed a man named Sayres and threw his body into the Willamette River. The police got wind of the murder and arrested him promptly. Bunko was sent to prison in Oregon.

The Shanghai Tunnels of Portland are open for tours to anyone brave enough to enter them. Visitors tell of being touched by cold, wet hands and hearing heavy footsteps.

Sometimes, they hear the sound of a chain rattle or smell the salty air from the sea. The ghosts that roam the dark tunnels are rumored to be the angry spirits of the men who had been shanghaied. Would you be brave enough to explore the haunted tunnels? Perhaps the ghost of Captain Bunko himself would greet you . . . and grab you to take you to his ship!

The Eerie Edgefield Hotel

The luxurious and amazing Edgefield Hotel in Troutdale, just fifteen miles from Portland, is something right out of a fairy tale. Once a run-down and neglected building, it has been brought back to its former glory. It sits on seventy-four acres of land and is surrounded by pretty vines, herb gardens, and outdoor fireplaces. The Edgefield is a massive redbrick building that has over one hundred guest rooms that one could easily get lost inside. It is nothing short of spectacular and extremely inviting, but maybe that is the reason it is haunted. The ghosts find it too wonderful to leave.

Built in 1911, the huge building was once a home for the poor. Many of these people never left; they stayed there until they died of old age. Today, several spirits wander the grounds and hallways. One ghost is a mother that lost her baby when it was just a few days old. The mom was so sad, she could not stop crying. People can hear her rocking her baby in a chair and singing nursery rhymes to soothe it back to sleep. Other times, they hear the poor mother crying and whimpering because she is so sad.

An old-time nurse still roams the halls, looking for patients. Her spirit wears an old-fashioned nurses' hat and white uniform. She carries a big bunch of keys and a cleaning bucket. One worker said she saw the phantom nurse and her wispy image walk right "through" her to the other side. She also felt an ice-cold chill as it happened! Other things that happen at Edgefield are ghosts yelling "Get out!," strange whispers in the hallways, and people being pushed by invisible hands.

The Ghost of a Fireman

Kell's Irish Pub on SW Second Avenue is a great place to stop in and grab a bite to eat. It has been around since 1983, but a certain ghost has been around much longer than that. It is a friendly ghost and one that is welcome to stay. His name is David Campbell, and he was a well-loved Portland fire chief since 1895. One day, on June 26, 1911, he was working near the old Union Oil Distribution Plant and started to smell smoke. He quickly ran to the fire to help anyone who might be trapped in the building. Unfortunately, it became he who was trapped in the flames. A loud explosion occurred, and smoke and metal surged high up into the air.

Fellow firefighters rushed to help Campbell, but he was already dead. Everyone mourned because he was so loved. Now his ghost lingers in the building known as Kell's Irish. Many visitors have seen Campbell standing near them, complete in his firefighting uniform and hat! He is always smiling. He sometimes gets bored and moves chairs, turns the television on and off, and plunks a few tunes on the piano in the basement. Some like to think that he is still watching over the people and his favorite city, Portland.

POPCORN AND GHOSTS AT THE HOLLYWOOD THEATER

It is rumored that remodeling a building will entice any spirits to make themselves known. This seems to be the case for the Hollywood Theater on NE Sandy Boulevard. Although many ghosts hang around the theater, a few stand out. The extravagant theater was built in 1926 and is the oldest running theater in the United States. It's very first film was a silent movie. Today, it can hold over fifteen hundred people and a large orchestra.

The most active spirit is a middle-aged and well-dressed man named Steve. He loves to hang out in the lobby. When paranormal investigators walked through the lobby, they said that Steve told them that he loved the Hollywood Theater, he had worked in the theater his whole life, and it meant everything to him. Unfortunately, he became sick and died.

Working at the Hollywood was the best thing he ever did, and he doesn't ever want to leave. He continues to roam the lobby and stairs. No one wants Steve to leave, so he will probably stay and watch movies for all eternity.

Lone Fir Cemetery

Nothing is creepier than a cemetery! Especially a cemetery that has over twenty-five thousand dead people in it. Lone Fir on SE Second Avenue is one of the largest and oldest cemeteries in Portland. Because of its age and the constant rain in Oregon, over ten thousand of the graves

had become unmarked, so no one knows exactly *who* is buried beneath the stones.

The most remarkable ghost is a girl named Emma Merlotin. She was born in France in 1885. She lived in a house on the corner of Third and Yamhill Streets in Portland. Emma was found in a pool of her own blood one night, bludgeoned to death by a stranger. Her roommate heard her laughing one minute and screaming the next. She ran downstairs, saw Emma, and called the police immediately.

The police arrived and found a creepy-looking man named William wandering outside. He had scratches on his face and bloody clothes. Suspicious, they arrested him. He lied and said the red stains were just paint, but it was blood. For some reason, they did not keep him in jail, and poor Emma's killer was never found. Reports of a female ghost in the graveyard are numerous. When you approach

the spirit, she throws up her hands, screams, and runs away. Is this the ghost of Emma still running from her killer?

The Lone Fir Cemetery hosts fun gatherings for Halloween, where it hired actors and hand out candy. If you go to the "Graveyard Goodies" event, maybe you will also see the ghost of Emma watching you!

Ghosts of the Coast

So far, you've read about ghosts galore, by land or by sea. Now, let's head further north along the Oregon Coast to see what other spirits await us!

THE GHOST IN THE LIGHTHOUSE

Tillamook, Oregon, is known for its cheese-making, crabbing, and beautiful beaches. It was named in 1891 after a local native tribe that lived in the area. But it is also known for the captivating lighthouse that bears its name, that still stands on a lonely rock out in the ocean, north of the town. Tillamook Rock Lighthouse can be seen from the beach of the Oregon Coast. The lighthouse was going to be built on Tillamook Head, a 15 million-year-old rock, but it would have been too hard and dangerous to construct. Instead, they chose to put the lighthouse nearby on a place simply called the "Rock."

While constructing the lighthouse, bad luck started from day one. The surveyor, Trewavas,

fell into the ocean and was never seen again. In 1880, over a dozen men were working on the lighthouse when a violent storm brewed. Everyone thought the men would be killed, but luckily, they survived. A year later, the ship *Lupatia* was sailing in thick fog, veered too close to the Rock, and struck it. *Lupatia* quickly sank to the bottom of the ocean floor and killed all sixteen men aboard. Four of the bodies were swept away by the waves and never found.

A lighthouse keeper named Gibbs was warned the place was haunted. He once saw a ghost ship, but when he called it in, no ship was ever found. It was rumored that the ghost of a former lighthouse keeper was jealous of the new men working there, and he would chase them around and make weird noises. The lighthouse is no longer in use, but it is still haunted!

Pirates, Ghosts, and Buried Treasure

Manzanita, Oregon, is a quaint coastal town nestled next to Neahkahnie Mountain. The name Manzanita means "little apple" in Spanish. Treasure hunters have been digging up the mountain for a very long time in the hopes of finding a buried treasure. Several hunters have been killed trying to locate the treasure, and many feel it is cursed.

A legend reveals a Spanish ship, possibly the *San Cristo de Burgos*, wrecked near the mountain in 1693. The surviving crew members loaded into a small boat and dragged a heavy chest onto the shore. The chest contained many jewels and gold. They dragged the chest

up the side of the mountain as the local Natives watched. The Natives watched the captain shoot his slave and bury him on top of the treasure. The captain knew the Natives would not dig up the chest since the dead man was now buried on top of it.

Many people have tried to find the buried loot, but none have been successful. The treasure is said to be protected by the soul of the murdered slave and anyone who tries will be cursed.

WATCH OUT FOR THE BANDAGE MAN

Cannon Beach, Oregon, is about the most beautiful place you will ever visit. The small town is bustling with millions of visitors every year. Bruce's Candy Kitchen is pure heaven; every inch of the small shop is packed with some sort of sugary delight. But if you are driving in a pick-up truck, you better beware! There is a legend that dates back to the 1950s of the ghost of a logger who got hurt on the job. He was bleeding all over, and he had gauze bandages all over his head and body to try to stop the blood.

He was quickly loaded into an ambulance and rushed off to the hospital, but it had been raining a lot at the coast, and the ground was soft and muddy. While en route to the hospital, the ambulance got struck by a mudslide. When help arrived, the injured logger had vanished!

People believe that the restless spirit of the logger, covered in bloody bandages from head to toe, is still trying to find his way to the hospital. Other visitors driving near the  area have seen him, too. They claim he likes to jumps into the bed of trucks. So, just where did the Bandage Man go? Did he die in the woods but nobody ever found him? Or is it just a creepy legend to scare people?

FRIGHTENING FORT STEVENS

During World War II in 1942, over 2,500 men were stationed at Fort Stevens. Just a few months after the attack on Pearl Harbor, all soldiers were still on high alert. The Japanese wished to complete a raid on US soil and used a long-range submarine. They fired at Fort Stevens, mistakenly thinking it was a submarine base. They did a lot of damage and injured many men at Fort Stevens.

Visitors still hear the echoes of the pain and suffering the soldiers endured, and they feel scared and nervous when exploring the fort. Many people see soldier ghosts dressed in Army uniforms hiding in the bunkers and bushes, still carrying their guns and swords. Are these ghosts dead soldiers killed during that war? Are they still trying to protect America? No one knows who the ghost soldiers are or why they are still stationed at Fort Stevens.

Today, you can explore the rusty remains of a real live shipwreck near the fort! The *Peter Iredale*, built in 1890, got into trouble when it encountered thick fog and a brutal storm. It was traveling from Mexico to Portland, Oregon. The large ship was pushed to shore in 1906, where it sank deep into the sand because it was so heavy. It is the *only* live shipwreck from the Graveyard of the Pacific that is assessable by land. It can be found at Fort Stevens State Park. Take your camera!

Astoria or "Ghostoria"?

Astoria is just one of the beautiful, coastal towns that are near the Graveyard of the Pacific. The entire town is so full of ghosts, it is hard to discover them all! The city of Astoria is the oldest in the State of Oregon. It met with disaster in 1883 when the entire town burnt to the ground. Over 2,500 people lost their homes and all their possessions. Luckily, only one person died in the flames. The city once again caught fire in 1922, causing serious damage. Today, the city is a lot of fun to visit and sightsee in. Perhaps you will run into a ghost or two!

A FREAKY FIRE STATION

The Uppertown Firehouse Museum is an interesting place to poke around and learn a few things about the history of firefighting. Located in Astoria on Marine Drive, it is an excellent way to learn about firefighting in the old days, how they used horses and carts, and what their uniforms looked like. The building is very old, built in 1896, so maybe that is why it is haunted! It started as a brewery where they make beer. That didn't work out, so it became a place to make milk. That didn't work out either. Finally, it was turned into a firehouse for the city in 1920 until it became a museum in 1990.

The building is haunted by two men, both ex-firefighters. They are in uniform, geared up, and ready to go! One spirit is a fireman who accidentally died while he was coming down the pole. The other man died when he was sleepwalking and fell to his death. People who visit the museum can hear someone walking around on the third floor when no one is up there. One of the ghosts likes to watch over people while they are napping. Both spirits are friendly and perhaps just enjoy hanging out at their old fire station.

Do you think the old ghosts would be amazed at how much the equipment has changed since they were firefighters? Maybe that is why they hang around, so they can learn about all the new procedures and fancy trucks!

THE TALE OF TWO MANSIONS

The Flavel family has long-time standing in the city of Astoria. Riverboat captain George Flavel made a lot of money running ships, so in 1884, he built his wife, Mary, and their three children, Kaye, Nellie, and his only son, George Conrad, a beautiful home. The mansion is almost 12,000 square feet with six fireplaces! Located on Eighth and Duane Streets, on a piece of land close to shore, it is one of the most spectacular homes in Astoria and looks like something out of a fairytale! The incredibly intricate-looking Queen Anne Victorian has three stories, lots of windows, and fancy woodwork. Captain Flavel loved the sea so much, he built a tall tower on the third floor so he could look out to the stormy ocean. From that high viewpoint, he could keep a watchful eye on any ships traveling through the Columbia River and was always on high alert in case he spotted trouble. And the tall windows also gave him a grand view over his favorite city, Astoria.

The first Flavel mansion is now a beautifully restored museum. On the main floor, visitors hear the soft tunes of a piano playing, laughter, and girls talking to each other when no one else is in the room. When Nellie was alive, she could play the piano skillfully, and was so good, she was often was asked to travel to Portland, Oregon, to play in concerts. Is the spirit of Nellie still playing her favorite songs on her piano?

In the living room, there resides an unhappy ghost. Why is it unhappy? Who does the upset spirit linger in the living room? No one knows.

On the second floor of the mansion, the ghost of a woman who floats through the rooms is seen often. But as soon as someone spots her, she quickly disappears without a trace! But the lingering scent of her floral perfume stays in the air.

Captain George Flavel spirit is seen in his old bedroom. He had piercing eyes; dark, thick hair; and a long beard and mustache. Flavel was one of the very first river bar pilots of the dangerous Columbia River and also one of Oregon's first millionaires! At just age thirty-one, he had become both wealthy and well-known. George became a local hero when he helped in the rescue of the sinking vessel SS *General Warren* in 1852. Flavel tried in vain to rescue everyone on board the massive ship during the wicked storm, but in the end, forty-two of fifty-two people drowned. Hundreds of pigs and chickens also lost their lives in the tragedy. Does the ghost of brave Captain George Flavel refuse to leave his home because he never wants to stop making sure ships cross the treacherous Columbia River safely?

The second grand Flavel mansion has an unpleasant past and an uncertain future. It is considered one of the most haunted houses in Oregon. The Colonial Revival–style manor is four stories high and, at one time, was one of the grandest homes in Astoria. It was built in 1901 for Captain George Flavel's son, George Conrad, and his wife, Wenona. It still stands today, a lonely reminder of the Favel fortune, on the corner of Fifteenth and Franklin.

When George died in 1923, he left the house to his son Harry Flavel, who lived there with his wife, Florence, and their two children, Harry and Mary. Harry earned the nickname "Hatchet Harry" when he locked his wife in a room upstairs. When neighbor Fred Fulton heard her screaming, he quickly ran over to help her. As he ran up the stairs toward Florence, Harry came running down carrying a hatchet! He hacked at the banister of the stairs in rage and threatened to kill Fred.

Thus, everyone in town started to call him "Hatchet Harry." Although trouble brewed inside the mansion, Harry did love dogs. He often stole people's dogs because he felt they were not taking good enough care of them. In 1983, Harry struck a car driving by him with a chain. When the angry man stopped his car to confront Harry, Harry stabbed him. After numerous trials and hearings, the Flavel family loaded up what they could in the car, along with a few dogs, and disappeared. Many claim that Hatchet Harry still haunts his old mansion, determined to keep people out.

LIBERTY THEATER

The extravagant Liberty Theater located on Commercial Avenue in Astoria is a place where one can see *more* than just performances.

It is haunted by a very good-looking ghost named Paul. The building started as the Weinhard-Astoria Hotel and was converted to a theater in 1925 after a horrible fire in 1922 that destroyed most of the city. In 1922, Astoria was devastated by flames. The Liberty Theater was the first building to be opened after the blaze. The new theater has twelve murals, ornate wood moldings, details, and intricate stained glass. The theater itself is so spooky, some can only stay there a few minutes before they run out scared to death! Is "Handsome Paul" an old actor or patron that performed or visited the theater when he was alive? Handsome Paul's spirit is seen wearing a white tuxedo and a straw Panama hat. He opens and closes doors and (when irritated) slams them!

MORE HAUNTED UNDERGROUND TUNNELS

After the horrible fire in Astoria in 1922, the new buildings were constructed 15 feet higher than the original city, which created hidden tunnels and alleys below. These tunnels are said to be haunted by the many men that the ruthless Jim Turk kidnapped to work on ships. Strange smells and loud noises can be heard coming from down in the depths of the tunnels.

Jim Turk ran a seaman's a cheap hotel for sailors on the south side of Commercial Street during the late 1800s. He was responsible for the shanghaiing of many men. Even ruthless Bunko Kelly considered Astoria to be dreadful. He said, "Astoria is the wickedest city in the world, even worse than New Orleans."

One man haunting the tunnels is a teenage worker named Richard Lewis. He was going about his business while walking home in the fog one evening when two men came up behind him and threw a coat over his head! Next thing Richard knew, he woke up on the floor in a wet, stinky tunnel. He was shoved over to the docks, pushed onto a ship, and forced to work. Perhaps his angry spirit is still trapped in the tunnels where he was beaten and kidnapped?

Kidnappers were prevalent in Astoria, and no one was safe from their crimes. Mont Hawthorne came to Astoria in the late 1800s, hoping to create a new life for himself. But he was warned of the captors, so he always carried his trusty gun on him.

One night, he was relaxing in his cabin when he was startled by the sounds of men trying to break down his front door! Frightened and remembering the warning he was told, he quickly grabbed his revolver and began shooting through the door. The abductors knew Hawthorne was not going to be taken prisoner easily, so they ran away. No one knows if Hawthorne's bullets hit any of them or not. One thing was sure: Hawthorne never went to bed without his revolver after that night!

Even the most innocent of men in Astoria were not safe. A kind Methodist minister named George Grannis almost fell victim to being kidnapped right in his church! On Sunday, before his sermon, preacher Grannis was ringing the bell to signal locals that it was time to make their way to the church. Out of nowhere, a dark overcoat was thrown over his head, and strangers grabbed him, pinning down his arms. But the strong minister fought back with all his might, even with his head covered up. He fought so hard that the men finally gave up and ran off! You can bet preacher George Grannis said an extra prayer that day for his fortunate escape from the kidnappers.

MEMALOOSE, ISLAND OF THE DEAD

Can you think of anything creepier than an island full of dead people? Memaloose Island, located along the Columbia River, is just that! The beautiful Columbia Gorge was once home to the Chinook Indian tribe, and they buried their dead in ritualistic ceremonies. The word *memaloose* came from the Chinook word *memalust*, or "to die." They placed their beloved in a canoe, set it on fire, and then shoved it off into the river or pulled it over to the island to be buried. They would chant prayers for their relative to make the journey to the next world safe and sound. They believed that sending the dead off to the nearby island would protect them from spirits that did not want to "leave" this world. They called these sacred places "islands of the dead."

One white man, Victor Trevitt, was a soldier in the Mexican War in 1846, where he lost one of his eyes. He later opened a toll bridge over the Deschutes River where he lived. Trevitt loved the Native Indians so much and had so much respect for them that his dying wish was to be buried with among them on Memaloose Island. When he died in 1883, he was buried as he wished, and a 13-foot-tall monument was erected in his honor.

But the Indian cemetery would not go undisturbed for long. In the late 1880s, a thief named James Hartley decided he would dig up the graves of the Indians' in search of beads, treasures, and artifacts. He had no respect for the dead. He looted many of the Indians grave vaults, stealing these sacred items from the tombs.

His bad deeds did not go unpunished, for he went missing in 1895. No one knew where he went until, finally, someone found his

body near Deadman's Lake. He had been tied up and placed in a canoe, and a stake was driven through his chest! Hartley now haunts the area.

In the 1930s, this sacred area of the Chinook Indians was disturbed again by travelers and explorers. Many feel these disturbances caused the dead to rise in protest and haunt the islands. Although Trevitt's grave was never disturbed, all of the Indians' graves (about 650 of them) had to be dug up and moved once the construction of the Bonneville Dam began in 1934. Their bodies were reburied in a safe spot nearby, but some say the souls of the disturbed Indians are angry and haunt whoever comes near their old graves.

CAPE DISAPPOINTMENT
AND DEADMAN'S HOLLOW

Cape Disappointment is a very scenic, coastal state park with cliffs overlooking the ocean, sandy beaches, and tall trees. The area was named by Captain John Meares in 1788, who was trying to find shelter at the opening of the Columbia River but was left "disappointed" when he could not find it, forcing him to move on. The nearby areas earned their names in the year 1853.

The large vessel *Vandalia* came to the area when it became trapped in the cape during a treacherous storm and began to break apart. It quickly sank to the bottom, taking all twelve men with it. Beard's Hollow earned its name when the body of Captain E.A. Beard, who was in charge of the *Vandalia,* washed ashore a few days later. The bodies of three other sailors were found on another nearby beach, which earned the name Deadman's Hollow. The bodies of the other eight men were never discovered. The wandering souls of all twelve men still linger on the salty shores of the cape.

All of the shipwrecks prompted the building of multiple lighthouses along the coastline. Two lighthouses were built in the vicinity: Cape Disappointment Lighthouse and the North Head Lighthouse. Today lighthouses are manned by an electronic beacon, but in the old days, men called lighthouse keepers had to live the harsh and lonely life of a keeper. The whipping 120 miles per hour winds and violent storms were extremely frightening and dangerous for the brave men that took these jobs.

One lighthouse keeper named Alexander Pesonen worked the North Head Lighthouse when he fell in love with a beautiful girl named Mary Watson. They married in 1890 and lived at the lighthouse, suffering the storms together. Mary tolerated the life of a lighthouse keeper's wife for

25 long years, but the gloomy weather, lack of outside communication, and harsh living conditions began to wear on Mary. In 1923, she was diagnosed with depression by a doctor in Portland. The next day, she decided to take a walk with her dog, Jerry. When Jerry returned to the lighthouse without Mary, Alexander became very worried!

They found Mary's coat lying in the grass on the bluff that towered 194 feet above the ocean's currents below. On a bank under the cliff lay Mary's corpse. No one knows of Mary accidentally fell or jumped from the cliff. Maybe the lighthouse life drove her to madness.

Her sad spirit has been seen lingering around the lighthouse and its grounds since 1950. Many believe Mary's ghost is looking for her beloved husband, Alexander.

Haunted Washington

As we carry on in our journey, we visit the great state of Washington, where more than a few ghosts like to make their presence known!

HAUNTED OFFICER'S ROW

A large city named Vancouver, Washington, is just over the river a few miles after you leave Portland, Oregon. It was named after Captain George Vancouver, who explored the Pacific

Northwest between the years 1791–1795. The nearby fort changed names a few times and was eventually called the Vancouver Barracks. The remains of an old fort, barracks, and officers' houses still stand and are an excellent day trip.

On the grounds, there is a row of magnificent mansions that the officers of the Army lived in. The military was stationed there to protect settlers who were coming here on the Oregon Trail from Indian attacks.

The haunted Grant House is a beautiful two-story structure with a fancy wrap-around porch on each level and elegant columns with an American flag on each one.

The ghost that haunts the Grant House is Lieutenant Colonel Alfred Sully. He lived at the house from 1874–1879 when he died. He likes to play games like locking doors and moving stuff around. One visitor said they heard his ghost say, "I lived here before and am just looking around."

In another house, the Nelson House, it is said that "blood" will sometimes ooze down the walls. No one knows why this creepy substance flows down the walls, but it is rumored that the wife of Admiral Paul Nelson spends hours trying to keep the walls clean! The grass in front of their house also does strange and unexplained things. Four days a week, the grass mysteriously changes from green to brown and then back again. The Nelson family tries to live with these bizarre occurrences and hopes someday they will just stop happening.

Nearby in barrack No. 614 (which used to be the old hospital for soldiers), people hear coughing, screams, and even laughter. Doors will open and close all by themselves. Even toilet lids move open and close for no reason.

Now, why would a ghost want to play with a toilet? No one knows. Perhaps it is the ghost of an old janitor who is still doing his job!

Ghostly Good Service

The city of Seaview was founded in 1880 by Johnathan Stout, who came to Washington from Ohio. The site became a regular stop for the passengers aboard the "Clamshell Railroad" as it made its route up the Long Beach Peninsula. The Shelburne Hotel opened in 1896 and is still operating today. Originally built by Charles Beaver, the handsome building had floor-to-ceiling stained-glass windows, intricate stairways, dark wood walls, and beautiful lighting.

While Mr. Beaver was helping with the construction of his hotel, he broke his arm, and it never healed properly, thus leaving him partially disabled. This became a frustration to him, as the heavy workload now fell upon his wife and daughter. Eventually, they were able to convince Charles to sell the hotel in 1911, which would allow them all an easier life. The spirit of Mr. Beaver still roams the hotel looking for items to repair or things to do. Properly working doors tend to lock themselves for no reason, and extreme temperature changes occur when the furnace is in good working order. Are these Mr. Beaver's ghosts trying to let the current owners know that he is still available to help out at his beloved hotel?

Rod's Lamplighter Restaurant and Lounge hosts a ghost named Katherine. She is always seen wearing the same long, white dress with puffy sleeves. Sometimes, her ghost accompanies the spirit of a man who always wears a black coat. Katherine was killed by a sea captain that she loved. No one knows why he killed her, but her ghost still roams the halls of the Lamplighter to this day.

The male spirit is former owner Louie Sloan, whose cremated ashes creepily are placed on a shelf in the restaurant. Lights flicker on and off, and pool billiard balls move around by themselves. The sounds of phantom footsteps are often heard. Sometimes, women feel their hair and face being touched by an invisible hand!

The Lions Paw Inn, built in 1911, was the first hospital on the Long Beach Peninsula. The ghostly presence of a nurse in cap and gown tends to enter rooms early in the morning as if still checking on her patients. In the upstairs

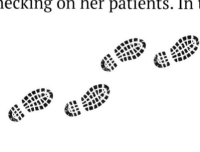

guest room, the ghost of a woman looking out the window can be seen from below. Who is she? Early in the morning, before anyone is up, the smell of bacon frying becomes overwhelming. But no one is cooking bacon!

A group of friendly ghosts can often be seen on the lawn playing a fun game of croquet together, all wearing clothes popular from a long time ago. Are these old pals wishing to keep the game going on for all eternity? Until they offer their names and information to someone, no one will ever know.

TOKELAND HOTEL AND THE GHOST OF CHARLEY

Visiting the Tokeland Hotel is like going back in time to the late 1800s, as not much has changed in the building since then. It is a large, rambling, three-story hotel where the guests share bathrooms (as was common in the old days) and also ghostly experiences! The Tokeland is the oldest active hotel in the State of Washington and a wonderful place to visit.

Tokeland was established in 1858 by George Brown and named after Chief Toke of the Shoalwater Bay Tribe. Brown and his daughter Lizzie built the hotel in 1885 and called it the Kindred Hotel. It is haunted by an old Chinese worker named Charley. He helped the owners out around the hotel but had to be very secretive because he had not legally entered the United States. If anyone found him, they would send him back to China. He built a secret hiding place in the large fireplace on the main floor by the dining room, where he would hide if he need to.

In 1930, he was hiding in the fireplace and accidentally suffocated. He was found dead, stuffed inside. Poor Charley still roams the halls of the Tokeland Hotel, helping out when he can. Stories of plates being tossed or "floating" above the tables, lights flickering on and off, and objects moving on their own are common.

The owners have witnessed many ghosts, including one woman—or at least half of her—who floats up the stairs and in the halls. She likes to lock people in rooms and jiggle doorknobs. There is also a phantom cat that loves to play and prowl in the Tokeland Hotel! But the most haunted room is No. 7, where a murder took place many years ago. The victim's spirit still seeks its killer all these years later.

THE GHOUL OF GRAYS HARBOR

A serial killer moved to the waterside town of Aberdeen in 1903, and unsuspecting sailors began losing their lives almost immediately. The killer was a man named Billy Gohl, and he killed over 100 men! Gohl did not like certain types of workers, and after he robbed them, he would kill them and toss their lifeless bodies into the Wishkah River near town of Grays Harbor. He would also kidnap men off ships. The bodies of men would be found floating in the water almost every day. Finally, Gohl was caught by the police and sent to jail. When they searched his cabin, they found several skulls!

A pub in Aberdeen named after the killer, Billy's Bar & Grill, houses the ghost of Billy Gohl. He tosses glasses across the bar when he feels mad. Employees have seen his ghost sitting in the bar drinking as if he was still alive. He is hard to miss as, he stood over six feet tall when he was alive!

PORT TOWNSEND'S GHOSTS

Port Townsend is one of the most beautiful and magical small seaport towns in the Puget Sound. And also the most haunted! Its towering Victorians and grand castles impress all who visit. Captain Henry Tibballs built an eccentric inn named the Palace Hotel on Water Street in 1856. It rises three stories tall and inside has 14-foot ceilings, velvet furniture, intricate woodwork, and fine paintings.

One of the ghosts in the Palace is featured in one of the paintings called *The Lady in Blue* whose real name was Claire. Her beautiful portrait hangs at the top of the stairs on the second floor. She roams the Palace freely, leaving the distinctive scent of her perfume wherever she goes. When she was alive, she lived in room No. 4. This is where she fell in love with a sea captain. She waited for him to return, but he never did. Some say she died of a broken heart. Guests have seen her from the street staring out her window that overlooks the water, still waiting for her captain's return. The muffled sounds of her crying late at night can be heard.

Another female ghost is named Miss Genevieve, who lived on the third floor. She is quite active and likes to knock pictures off the walls, create scary shadows, and even levitate beds off the floor! Some people refuse to work on the third floor because they never want to see a ghost.

Some claim that the spirit of Mr. Tibballs himself still roams his grand hotel, checking on guests and making sure everything is absolutely perfect!

Another Port Townsend haunt is the Victorian-style Ann Starrett Mansion. Truly magnificent in its architecture, the mansion is considered the "grandest of them all!" It has an eight-sided domed tower that is said to be haunted by Ann herself, as it was her favorite room on the huge place. George fell in love with Ann in 1893 and spared no expense while building a home for them. He loved her so much that he promised they would be together forever, and they are certainly keeping that promise! Their apparitions can be seen together, still holding hands and admiring their beautiful home. Even their red-haired nanny loves the home so much, she refuses to leave, too! She is the most active and doesn't hesitate to thump a guest on the head if she doesn't like something they do or say!

A Very Scary Castle

Manresa Castle was built in 1892 to replicate a fine three-story European castle, complete with a fancy turret and thirty rooms. Charles Eisenbeis, who came to Port Townsend in 1858, wanted to build the biggest mansion in town, so he did. One ghost that remains in the castle is that of English Kate. In 1921, she fell in love with a man who was out at sea. She stayed at the castle waiting for his return but got word that his ship had sunk. In distress, she tossed herself out the window of room No. 306! This is said to be the most haunted of all the thirty rooms in Manresa. Sadly, her love did not die in the shipwreck, but it was too late for poor Kate. Her spirit now remains at the castle, still feeling guilty for taking her own life in such haste. Today, she amuses herself by going through guests' belongings, looking at their jewelry and shoes. Her lovely voice can be heard in the middle of the night as she sings softly to herself. She will create both good odors and bad, depending on whether she likes a guest or not.

A second ghost is a Jesuit priest who fell in love with a woman in town. He was so ashamed of himself that he hung himself from a rafter in a room in the attic above room No. 302. The sound of him pacing back and forth above the room is often heard by guests sleeping below, and if people try to contact the young priest, he recites bible verses back to them.

Strange and Spoooky Seattle

Seattle is one of the largest cities in the United States, and it goes on for miles and miles when viewing it! Settlers came to the area in 1851 when it was inhabited by Natives. The pioneers wanted to call it New York but changed their minds and instead called it Seattle to honor Chief Seattle.

Below Seattle is a vast network of tunnels, some hidden, some not. After the great fire of 1889 that destroyed most of the city, the townspeople decided to rebuild Seattle up twelve feet, which created the tunnels. Ghost tours are about the only way to get access to these spooky passageways. The most encountered spirit is a tall man who has a handlebar mustache and wears suspenders and a top hat. His name is Edward, and he worked as a teller in the old bank during the late 1890s. Back then, the bank would allow withdrawals anytime, day or night. Edward was killed in a shootout while he was working at the bank. Some people even claim to have held conversations with Edward's ghost!

The ghost of a woman who was also killed at the bank is often seen. She was hiding behind the bank's vault when she was killed. Her ghostly image has been captured in photographs, and tourists claim to have seen orbs and felt cold spots anytime she appears.

ROOM #408

The beautiful Italian-style Sorrento Hotel was built in 1909 by Samuel Rosenberg to offer a view of both the water and the city. It is not only the oldest hotel in Seattle, but also the most haunted!

The female ghost that roams the halls is Alice Toklas. She loves to move people's drinks and play games. Her image can be seen wearing white or black, floating downstairs or behind the bar. Alice moved to Seattle in 1890 to study music at the university. She especially loved playing the piano. In the Penthouse Suite, guests hear the piano play when no one is there.

Her family used to own the land that the Sorrento is built on. After the hotel was built, she would stay in her favorite room every time she visited Seattle, room No. 408. But why does Alice haunt the Sorrento? It is another Seattle mystery. One thing is certain: Alice has no plans on leaving.

CREEPY KELLS

Kells Irish Pub is located in the Butterworth Building on First Avenue. It is also built over an old mortuary! Kells is the most haunted pub in America and the home to two ghosts. In 1903, the Butterworth & Sons Mortuary has a thirty-coffin room and an elevator for moving the dead bodies from the basement to the upper level. Today, visitors enter the restaurant through the very same door that the dead used to enter through!

Charlie (why are so many ghosts named Charlie?) haunts Kells and is an older gentleman always seen wearing a derby hat. And he *loves* music! Every time the bar hosts live music, Charlie is right there next to the band. He is a very friendly and happy ghost.

A real live Haunted House

Ever wanted to visit a real-life haunted house? The Georgetown Morgue on Marginal Way South offers just that! Be prepared to be completely freaked out, if you dare. Since 1928, the building was once a mortuary where thousands of people had their funerals. The hauntings started in 1947, when a former Seattle Jazz trumpeter named John "Figgy" Dorsey was being prepared for his funeral. Much to the employee's surprise, his body disappeared! It was later found in the front yard of his home. His wife was so tortured by

this event that she killed herself. His ghost is seen wandering the mortuary where his body was stolen, and sometimes the faint sound of his trumpet can be heard.

In 1965, a man named Charles (another Charlie!) died in the building during an earthquake. His restless spirit still roams the halls, looking for an escape. A horrible unsolved crime occurred in the building when nine employees were murdered. The killer was never found. Some say the ghosts of these nine people still search for their killer. Today, the haunted building offers escape games and other ghostly activities.

Haunted British Columbia

Finally, we have crossed the border into Canada to pay a visit to the ghostly spirits of British Columbia! We begin in Victoria, one of the oldest cities in the Pacific Northwest and considered by many to be the most haunted city in Canada!

GHOSTS OF AN OLD CITY

The City of Victoria was founded in 1843. The beautiful, historic waterfront city is bustling with tourists and locals and also filled with ghosts! The most haunted part of Victoria is a section known as Bastion Square, located in the Old Town part of the city.

Bastion Square is plagued by the ghosts of prisoners from the 1800s who were once held captive in the jail, waiting to be hanged. One spirit in particular that haunts the Square is a man who was beaten to death by a prison guard. Sounds of dragging chains and clanking

metal can be heard when his ghost appears. The local pub, Garrick's Head (located across the street from the old courthouse), was where prisoners would eat their very last meal and drink their last pint of beer before dying. All of the tortured souls of the men hanged still roam the streets late at night.

The most popular ghost in town is the old pub owner, Mike Powers, who bought the pub in 1899. He was brutally murdered on October 1 that same year. As Mike was unlatching his gate, two attackers hit him over the head with a sandbag. Once he hit the ground, they continued to kick and beat him until they thought he was dead. Mike survived another four painful days until he died of a ruptured liver. His assailants were never caught.

Mike's ghost still enjoys sitting by the same wood-burning fireplace in his pub, as he did over 120 years ago.

THE GREY LADY IN McPHERSON PLAYHOUSE

The McPherson Playhouse was built in 1914 and has entertained guests for over 100 years. Up in the balcony lurks the ghost of a woman the actors simply call the "Grey Lady." She hangs around the theater mostly at night, and although her spirit is said to be friendly, she does tend to scare everyone! Night janitors refuse to be alone in the building, and many have quit their jobs because the Grey Lady frightens them. The playhouse installed "ghost lights" that keep the balcony lit and hopefully keep the Grey Lady away.

VICTORIA'S CREEPY CEMETERIES

The old cemetery (that served the public from 1855–1873) is now Pioneer Square, and a whopping 1,300 people are buried there. But they are not at rest. When the city decided to make the cemetery into a park in 1908, it removed the headstones! The angry spirits haunt the cemetery in protest.

One ghost is the "White lady of Langley Street." Her name is Adelaide Griffin, and she died in the 1850s. Adelaide and her husband, Ben, opened up the Boomerang Saloon across from the old jail. Whenever there was a public hanging, their saloon was very busy. Adelaide died suddenly and was buried at the old cemetery. Her image can be seen every Christmas Eve at the site of her beloved Boomerang Saloon.

Robert Johnson's spirit also lingers. In the 1870s, he slit his own throat, committing suicide. His tortured soul is seen in the cemetery often, reenacting his final moments.

In Victoria's Ross Bay Cemetery, many ghosts roam the grounds. The most notorious spirit is of David Fee. Fee was murdered on Christmas Eve 1890 as he was leaving St.

Andrews Cathedral on his way to a Christmas party. As he walked down the steps, wearing a white raincoat, a man came up behind him and shot him! The killer, Lawrence Phelan, discovered he had shot the wrong man and confessed to the police. He intended to kill an enemy who also wore a white raincoat. Strangely, Fee's body was moved to the

Christmas party anyway, his bloody corpse propped up in a chair. The spirit of Fee is seen on Christmas Eve at two locations: the Ross Bay Cemetery and on the steps at St. Andrews where he was killed. He is always wearing his blood-stained white coat.

Conclusion

I hope you have enjoyed our stories about the Pacific Northwest and all the ghouls and ghosts that make these interesting places their homes. Maybe someday you will encounter a ghost yourself, and you can tell your very own scary story!